Marriage - A Melody

Swami Tejomayananda

Central Chinmaya Mission Trust

First Edition - April 2012 - 5,000 copies
Reprint - December 2012 - May 2016 - 15,000 copies
Reprint - January 2020 - 2,500 copies

Published by:
Chinmaya Prakashan
The Publications Division of
Central Chinmaya Mission Trust
Sandeepany Sadhanalaya
Saki Vihar Road, Powai, Mumbai 400072, India
Tel.: +91-22-2803 4900
Email: ccmtpublications@chinmayamission.com
Website: www.chinmayamission.com

Distribution Centre in USA:
Chinmaya Mission West
Publications Division
560 Bridgetown Pike
Langhorne, PA 19053, USA
Tel.: 1-888-CMW-READ, (215) 396-0390 Fax: (215) 396-9710
Email: publications@chinmayamission.org
Website: www.chinmayapublications.com

Designed by: Chinmaya Kalpanam, Mumbai

Printed by: Usha Multigraphs Pvt. Ltd., Mumbai

ISBN 978-81-7597-534-7

Publisher's Note

Distress filled marriages and stress filled parenting have become common maladies of present times. As an antidote to them Chinmaya Mission, Ann Arbor, USA organised a two day seminar for young couples on *Marriage – A Melody* in July 2009 which was addressed by Pūjya Gurujī and Acāryā Vilasini.

Pūjya Gurujī through his unique compositions in song and verse (refer *Life of Vision* and *Tips for Happy Living*) and his talks, elaborated on topics like secret of a successful marriage, purpose of marriage, harmony in relationships and tips on happy parenting. He also answered questions by the participants.

These talks were transcribed by Kum. Tulsipriya Goyal, Delhi and first edited by Smt. Mita Samani, London. The book was designed and edited by members of Chinmaya Kalpanam and Chinmaya Prakashanam. CCMT Publication Department Thanks to all for creating this melody in words.

We pray that it brings greater rhyme and rhythm in the marriages of all who tune in to its wisdom.

Central Chinmaya Mission Trust
Mumbai - 400 072

Transliteration and Pronunciation Guide

In this book, Devanagari characters are transliterated according to the scheme adopted by the International Congress of Orientalists at Athens in 1912. In it one fixed pronunciation value is given to each letter; f, q, w, x and z are not called to use. According to this scheme:

Devanagari	Translit-eration	Sounds Like	Devanagari	Translit-eration	Sounds Like
अ	a	son	ढ्	ḍh	adhesive*
आ	ā	father	ण्	ṇ	under*
इ	i	different	त्	t	tabla
ई	ī	feel	थ्	th	thumb
उ	u	full	द्	d	this
ऊ	ū	boot	ध्	dh	Gandhi
ऋ	ṛ	rhythm*	न्	n	nose
ॠ	ṝ	**	प्	p	pen
ऌ	ḷ	**	फ्	ph	phantom*
ए	e	evade	ब्	b	boil
ऐ	ai	delight	भ्	bh	abhor
ओ	o	core	म्	m	mind
औ	au	now	य्	y	yes
क्	k	calm	र्	r	right
ख्	kh	khan	ल्	l	love
ग्	g	gate	व्	v	very
घ्	gh	ghost	श्	ś	shut
ङ्	ṅ	ankle*	ष्	ṣ	sugar
च्	c	chuckle	स्	s	simple
छ्	ch	witch*	ह्	h	happy
ज्	j	justice	ं	ṁ	improvise
झ्	jh	Jhansi	ः	ḥ	**
ञ्	ñ	banyan	क्ष्	kṣ	action
ट्	ṭ	tank	त्र्	tr	three*
ठ्	ṭh	**	ज्ञ्	jñ	gnosis
ड्	ḍ	dog	ऽ	'	a silent 'a'

* These letters don't have an exact English equivalent. An approximation is given here.

** These sounds cannot be approximated in English words.

We take the opportunity to thank
Smt Pankajalata Rath and Shri Udayanath Rath
for having sponsored the printing of
this book and ensuring that this timeless
wisdom reaches the hands of seekers galore.

Contents

Marriage - A Melody

Congratulations!!

Greetings on your wedding/wedding anniversary day!

विवाहदिनमिदं भवतु हर्षदम् ।
मङ्गलं तथा वां च क्षेमदम् ॥१ ॥

vivāhadinamidaṁ bhavatu harṣadam,
maṅgalaṁ tathā vāṁ ca kṣemadam. (1)

1. May this wedding day bring to both of you happiness, auspiciousness and well-being.

प्रतिदिनं नवं प्रेम वर्धताम् ।
शतगुणं कुलं सदा हि मोदताम् ॥२ ॥

pratidinaṁ navaṁ prema vardhatām,
śataguṇaṁ kulaṁ sadā hi modatām. (2)

2. Day by day, may you discover new love for each other. May it grow a hundredfold and may your family ever rejoice.

लोकसेवया देवपूजनम् ।
गृहस्थजीवनं भवतु मोक्षदम् ॥३॥

lokasevayā devapūjanam,

gṛhastha-jīvanaṁ bhavatu mokṣadam. (3)

3. Through service to people, as worship of God, may your household life lead you to Liberation.

Make It Happen

The world population is very large. Among the billions in this world you could have married, you chose your particular spouse. You may have married for a variety of reasons. It could have been a love marriage, arranged marriage or a combination of the two. But the fact is that you are now married. It is said that 'marriages are made in heaven' but to maintain them, is your responsibility. You may have to work at making your marriage a success. It will not happen automatically.

There are some people who 'make things happen', others 'talk of things that have happened' and yet others just wonder, 'what happened!' You must belong to the first category. You have to make the marriage work, even when you face various challenges and problems which are given freely and generously by the world.

Making It Happen

In life we may know a lot, but doing what we know is important. 'Knowing is not doing, doing is doing', says Pūjya Śrī Gurudev Swami Chinmayananda.

Sometimes outwardly a couple may look happy – partying and vacationing, but between them there is stress and conflict. Marriage should bring to your life joy, auspiciousness and well-being. All three are important. Married life must be full of joy – not just thrills – but cheer and lightness, fun and brightness. There must also be a sense of 'well-being' – being good and well with each other. There must also be auspiciousness – a purity and beauty in your relationship.

Healthy and Wealthy

A lifestyle of simple living and high thinking brings joy and peace. Avoid extremes – indulgence or deprivation, overeating or extreme dieting, working to the bone or indolence, thinking too much or no thinking, extreme attachment or hatred. A balanced life keeps us physically and mentally healthy and health truly is our wealth. So a healthy and wealthy life does bring joy and well-being.

Responsibility

The word 'vivāha' (marriage) comes from the Sanskrit verbal root 'vah' which means 'to carry'. It means to take on the special responsibilities that go with married life.

The first responsibility is to make the marriage a success. The second responsibility is to support and take care of the immediate and extended family along with dispensing social and national responsibilities. As you perform your duties, you earn the right to enjoy the fruits of your hard work.

This stage of life is called the gṛhastha-āśrama literally meaning 'dwelling at home' (gṛha + stha). The other three stages are called brahmacarya (student life), vānaprastha (retired life) and sannyāsa (life of renunciation). In the ancient days, students lived in residential schools or colleges (gurukulas), retired people lived in forest or hermitage and the sannyāsins or monks lived in hermitages or were wandering. The householder stays at home and takes the responsibility of supporting the others and is therefore very important for the sustenance and maintenance of society.

Secret of Successful Marriage

Someone remarked that everyone wants to know the secret of a successful marriage but no one knows it, since it is a very well-kept secret! However I believe that it is quite well-known but not so well practised. It is – 'discover new love and respect for each other and let them grow each day'.

Love 'before marriage' is common but love 'after marriage' is more important. Trust strengthens love. Unobstructed by doubt and mistrust, love matures and grows. Fed by renewed feelings of tenderness, care and concern, love is nourished and blossoms. Love should never become stale and its expression gross, routine or mechanical.

We respect the person when we see what we value in them. The more we value what others have, the more we shall respect them. Thus ever increasing mutual love and respect is the secret of a successful marriage.

Love and Attachment

Attachment pollutes the pure flow of love. You should understand the difference between the two. When you love someone, you want to make the other person happy. You serve selflessly and tirelessly and take joy in loving and giving. In attachment you want to make yourself happy. Love gets polluted by demands and expectations, possessiveness, jealousy and insecurity.

When you love each other 'because of' something then if that cause goes away, the love also vanishes. A girl asked her fiancé, "Do you love me because my father will give me a lot of money?" The boy replied, "Of course not! I will love you even if your wealthy uncle will give you the money!" Real love is to love 'in spite of' any external circumstances or differences. Changing situations cannot rock a stable marriage anchored on mutual love. The fleeting cannot sweep away the lasting bond of true love.

The Higher Purpose of Marriage

We should be very clear about the goal of every action we undertake. Most of us are vague or confused about it, have given little thought to it or have superficial goals. A young boy was asked why he went to college. He said, "Without a degree, no girl will marry me!" Another person who was asked why he got married, answered, "It was not a willful act. It happened so suddenly that one day I just found myself married!"

The teacher asked the student in her carpentry class, what he was making. "A portable", he replied. The confused teacher asked, "A portable what?" He said, "I have not thought about that yet. I have made a handle and everything portable has a handle!" This is like saying, "I have already got married, now let me find out its purpose".

The Immediate and Long Term Goals of Marriage

To make your marriage successful and joyful you must have an inspiring and lasting goal. The immediate goal must be geared towards something more permanent. The short term needs must lead to the fulfilment of the long term goals. For example, a student studies well to join the medical college (immediate goal) in order to become a doctor and serve mankind (long term goal).

For those whose immediate goal of having fun becomes their only long term and ultimate goal, their pleasures end in pressures – blood pressure, family, social and economic pressures! If marriage is only taken as a permit for licentious living or pleasure seeking without family or social responsibility, it will not be a happy marriage nor will it last. When it is geared towards something inspiring and permanent, it will bring stability, peace, growth and happiness.

Many people make New Year resolutions, particularly about losing weight and keeping fit. In early January there is a sudden increase in membership in health clubs and gyms (weight loss is a loss which is actually a gain!) but in a few days' time the resolve dissolves and weight gain wins over weight loss. A man stood on the weighing scale one day and called out to his wife, "Come here quickly, you know all that weight that I had lost. Well, I found it here!"

Contrast this with a person whose goal is to win a gold medal in the Olympics. He enthusiastically exercises and controls his diet on a regular and sustained basis. Since the goal is something higher, nobler and more permanent, his actions become a means to achieve it. In this case, the discipline in life is abiding and permanent and his actions and life become more meaningful and focused.

Then should not the married couple have any ambitions of material prosperity and comfort or for name, fame and power in society? Yes, you can have such immediate goals and work hard to achieve them. However the purpose of earning wealth should not be merely for your own pleasure and prosperity, but to serve others in whatever capacity you can.

Serve others through your wealth, talents and profession. One with a good voice can sing for others. A lawyer, doctor, scientist or sportsperson can benefit society through their hard work. Do not only think how much the profession can benefit you, but also think how much you can contribute to the profession, how you can serve others through your profession. Be an ideal lawyer or doctor. A still higher attitude is to make your work a worship of God, 'service of the Lord of Lords and devotion to people as devotion to the supreme Self' (Chinmaya Mission Pledge).

Marriage is an opportunity to serve others. Start with your spouse and extend this service to your immediate and extended family, friends and society. Think constantly about how you can contribute to the prosperity and well-being of others. The world gives us enough opportunities to serve. Be alert and ready to serve. When service becomes your goal and a habit, your life and work become inspired, selfless and joy-giving and your mind becomes pure and peaceful. You will become less egoistic and selfish and your insistences, likes and dislikes will reduce. Such a pure mind will take you to greater heights of material and spiritual success.

Purity of Mind

Why should we aim for a pure mind? A pure mind is cheerful, peaceful, alert, strong and focused. It can achieve anything and everything. It is achieved through serving others with the right attitude and following values in life. Most people have respect for values like honesty but are unable to live them.

A question arises – 'Why should I be honest?' If the purpose of honesty in business is to build a good reputation and attract customers, then it will last till the business has gained a reputation, after which the temptation for dishonesty will arise again. However when you realise that honesty makes me happy and dishonesty brings stress and sorrow, we will be honest not just for the immediate benefit, but for a more lasting goal, to purify our mind and prepare it for still higher goals.

Liberation – The Ultimate Goal of Life

In the student life our goal is to study and empower ourselves. The monk (sannyāsi) is supposed to have only a spiritual goal – seek God/Liberation. The householder can have material goals for fulfilling material needs and also aim to serve others. These goals prepare you with a pure mind to achieve the highest spiritual goal of Liberation.

What is Liberation? It is freedom from all bondages. It includes freedom from the slavery to all objects, senses and the mind. Are you bound? Most of us feel we are not. We feel we can give up drinking tea any time we want to and so it is not a binding habit.

But can we really? This we can test by actually giving it up. Test your attachment to watching TV by switching off and walking away from the TV in the middle of your favourite TV serial. How much you miss it, crave for it, depend on it or are possessive of it, shows how much you are attached to an object, being or situation. If you can painlessly give up (not by substituting it with another object), then you are a master and if not, you are beholden to it. Then you don't own it, it owns you. So be a householder, but do not hold on to the house. Do not become enslaved by pleasures.

The highest understanding of Liberation is to give up false identification with the body, senses and mind and realise the Truth – to know that I am not the perishable body but eternal and infinite Existence. This is also called God-realisation or Self-knowledge. Married life should prepare you to reach this highest goal of human life.

Sometimes people ask what svāmīs would know about married life. Someone jokingly answered that the very fact that they did not marry shows that they know. Yes, there are lots of challenges. You will have to overcome a lot of conflicts, challenges and problems that come in married life. One piece of advice may help. Make it a rule to resolve each day's quarrels or differences before you sleep. At least agree to disagree and sleep on a positive note. Also, do not keep awake all night attempting to resolve the problem.

Marriage is not just a social obligation, a familial duty, a mutual need or a legal agreement and definitely not a commercial deal. It is a sacred relationship, a coming together of two souls and two families. Do not allow any challenges and obstacles to break it and work hard to make it a success. Invoke God's grace and Guru's blessings for spiritual strength. Success is guaranteed with grace and right effort. God bless you all.

Harmony in Relationships

Man is a social being and cannot live in isolation. Even those renunciates who live in a cave have to mingle with others to procure food. It is natural to form relationships. They are like a mirror and show us what we are.

Staying in a cave I may claim to have conquered anger. This will be tested only when I am with someone and when I am provoked by that person. Someone asks me what my name is? I may say, "Jitakrodhānanda" – one who has conquered anger. "But I don't believe so, what proof do you have?" he asked. I shout back and say, "How dare you question me?" Interaction with others tests our relationships and reveals to us what we are.

Some people have difficulties and some people are difficult. Interestingly, each one thinks that the other is very difficult to live with or deal with. Why are relationships difficult to manage? Why do they turn sour, become unhealthy, are problematic and binding or cause suffering and tension? Why are many people in the family just tolerating each other, waiting to quit or breaking up?

Here are a few tips which will help us to live in harmony with others –

(1) 'If the basis of any relationship is worldly, then it is binding. But if it is spiritual then it is liberating'.[1]

If a boy marries a girl for her riches and her riches dwindle, the relationship ends. If he marries her for her beauty and the beauty fades away, then he too turns away. If she marries him for his power and fame and he loses them, she may lose her respect for him.

Love others for what they are and not just for what they have. Love others not 'because of' their material possessions but 'in spite of' them. Material

[1] *kasyacidapi sambandhasya-ādhāro yadi laukikas-tarhi sa bandhana-kāraka, ādhyātmikastu mukti-dāyako bhavati.* – *Jivansūtrāṇi 5.5*

things come and go. If you love others for their virtues or in spite of what they are, the love will be firm.

Always ask, 'What is the basis of my relationship?' even with material things. If you consider money only as a means to purchase power, fame and pleasures, then it will cause pride, attachment and stress. When you think it to be God-given, you will remain humble and relaxed. When you understand that money will not remain forever, today it is in my pocket, tomorrow it will be in another's. The *Iśāvāsya-upaniṣad* says, 'Do not hoard wealth. To whom does it belong anyway'. It is meant for sharing and helping others. With this attitude money will become a blessing for yourself and others and not cause conflicts and sorrows.

Śrī Gurudev Swami Chinmayananda says, 'What you have is God's gift to you and what you do with what you have, is your gift to Him'. This attitude will bring you joy. When the thing goes, you will think that the Lord decided you do not need it anymore. When the thing remains you will share it with others like prasāda (His gift).

Our relationship with God also breaks down when it is based on worldly desires alone. We feel that He should fulfill all our worldly desires and if He does not, we lose faith and leave Him.

Remember always – God is not just your wish-fulfiller; but also your well-wisher. Like a mother who denies her sick child ice cream, even though he screams for it, God does what is good for you not just what you think what is good for you. Sometimes He says, 'yes' and gives you what is 'good' for you. Sometimes He says, 'no' and gives you what is 'better'. Sometimes He says, 'wait' and gives you the 'best'. So have faith in His goodness and wisdom and your relationship with Him will remain steadfast.

Plants and animals can live happily without us but we cannot survive without them. If our attitude is that they are meant for our pleasure, to do what we want with them, we will destroy them. When we consider ourselves to be the 'big brother' of creation, we will take care and nourish them and they in turn will flourish and benefit.

A parable in the *Bible* says that if you build a house on shifting sands then storms will easily wash it away but if you build it on a rock then it stands strong, like a lighthouse in the ocean. So let the basis of your relationship with material objects, plants, animals, human beings, Guru or God be spiritual, based on ideals and values, then it will remain well rooted and long lasting.

(2) 'One should look upon people as one's own Self but do not consider them to be like oneself' and 'One should not impose one's ideas of joy, sorrow etc. on others and should give them freedom'.[1]

'Do unto others as you would have others do unto you' is the basis of harmonious relationships. I love myself and want all to love me unconditionally – so do others. I like my space and freedom and so do others. I have my ideas of what gives joys and sorrows and others do so too. If we think that everyone thinks like us or that they should think like us, then there will be friction and unhappiness.

When you seek to please others, try and find out what they want, how they think. A boy came home and happily declared, "Daddy, I helped an old lady

---

[1] *ātmavallokān-paśyen-na tu tathā bhāvayet. sukha-duḥkhādi-viṣayaka-sva-kalpanām-anyasmin-nāropayet. tebhyaḥ svātantryaṁ prayacchet.* – *Jīvansūtrāṇi 5.6-7-8*

cross the road today". The father said, "She must have been happy". "No", said the boy, "She got very mad because she did not want to cross". Doing good work is good. But not just according to your own ideas, likes or dislikes. Respect others' needs and ideas as well.

The problem is more acute in close relationships like between husband and wife as there is maximum expectation and possessiveness. The husband and wife love each other and even try to make each other happy but strangely they often do not try to find out what the other wants! Men and women think differently and also express their love differently. When he expresses love in his own way she is not happy and thinks he does not love her. So look upon everyone as your own Self, but also know that each individual is unique and you respect their freedom to think differently and try to understand them.

(3) 'People should be respected and trusted, not suspected'.[1]

Respect and trust people you are living with. In the beginning your relation should be based on

---

[1] *janā ādaraṇīyā viśvasaniyā na tu śaṅkanīyāḥ. – Jīvansūtrāṇi* 5.1

mutual trust and not on suspicion, then alone will true love develop in due course.

Some suspect everyone. If someone invites you for dinner, you start to doubt and question. You think, 'There is no free lunch, so they must want something from me'. If the other person just smiles, you think, 'why is he smiling?' and if he does not smile, then again you are suspicious. This doubting nature pollutes the relationship. Such a person is always disturbed and agitated. 'A 'doubting person' destroys himself' says the *Gītā* (saṁśayātmā vinaśyati). Start the relationship on trust. Just because one person has betrayed you, that does not mean all will do so. Also a person who has cheated once may regret what he has done and he could have changed for the better. Do not always be suspicious. Trust others, even if it is for your own peace of mind. Our peace of mind is most precious. Do not squander it away through suspicions. Trust yourself and trust others.

(4) 'One should be strict with one's own faults but be tender towards others' (faults)'.[1]

---

[1] *svadoṣānprati kaṭhoro'nyeṣām prati tu komalo bhavet. – Jīvansūtrāṇi 5.2*

You are not perfect. You too have many faults. You want others to accept you as you are, but you do not accept the faults of others. If you are jealous, then you think that being jealous is not so bad but being angry like the other person is terrible. We usually justify and are tender towards our own faults and are strict, unforgiving and condemning towards the faults of others. However we should be just the opposite if we are to have harmonious relationships. Be tender towards others' faults and strict towards your own faults.

Mahātmā Gandhi said that because you also are imperfect, forgive others. The wise men say that because you are perfect, forgive the faults of others. Some people think they are perfect and expect perfection from others. A perfectionist is never liked by others. He is defined as one who takes a lot of pain and distributes it to others.

Be understanding of the limitations and difficulties of others. Be compassionate and kind to them. I visited a house where I saw a poster that said, 'Don't try and change me. Accept me as I am!' However, if we are not strict towards our own faults, we will never change for the better and in time we will even glorify our fault saying, 'So what if I get angry. It gets the work done'. Our dūṣaṇa (fault) should not be considered as our bhūṣaṇa (glory).

(5) 'If there is mutual love and trust, then rules and regulations are not needed. In their absence also rules are not needed as they do not work'.[1]

When there is love and trust between a couple, there is no need to write down job profiles, duty lists, working hours, specific working conditions, privileges, bonuses and so on. Parents do not tell their children to fall sick only before 10.00 p.m because after that their duty time is over! But when relationships are strained and divorce proceedings are on, rules are made about visiting hours and sharing of property. But these rules do not really make things easier or relationships better or anyone happier. In an organisation which respects its staff, many people are happy to work day and night. When there is a negative feeling, however many bonuses are given, there is dissatisfaction

[1] *pārasparika-sneha-viśvāse vartamāne vidhi-niyamā anāvaśyakāḥ. avidyamāne'pi anāvaśyakā yato niṣphalāḥ.* – *Jīvansūtrāṇi 5.3-4*

and disturbance and relationships are strained and productivity is affected.

So, for harmony in relationships, its basis must be spiritual. If the relationship has a material or superficial foundation, it will crumble. But when relationships are based on a firm foundation of virtues, they are strong, lasting and a source of joy.

Joy of Parenting

Amongst the various joys of married life, parenting, especially when the child is young is the most joy giving. However it can also become quite challenging. Someone was once speaking on stress-free parenting. He said, 'Parenting is always stress free. It brings stress, free of charge'. A man once joked that before marriage he had six theories on how to raise children. Now he has six children and no theories.

Here are a few verses composed by me on parenting which could help you make parenting truly joyful.

जयति तेऽधिकं बालजन्मना भवनशोभनं हर्षपूरितम्।
प्रभुकृपाफलं स्पष्टगोचरम् अवसरे शुभे तेऽभिनन्दनम् ॥१॥

jayati te'dhikaṁ bālajanmanā bhavana-śobhanaṁ harṣa-pūritam,
prabhu-kṛpā-phalaṁ spaṣṭa-gocaram avasare śubhe te'bhinandanam. (1)

1. 'The joy at the birth of your child has further beautified your beautiful home. It is the clear manifestation of God's grace. Congratulations to you on this auspicious occasion'.

A child's birth fills the house with joy. There is great joy and expectation even before its birth. Nowadays parents want to see the child even when it is in the womb. Once the child is born every expression, movement and mood is watched, talked about and photographed. 'He opened his eyes', 'He looked at me' and 'He smiled'... what else will the baby do?

The child's birth should be considered not just as a biological process or as attaining 'parenthood'. We should see it as the grace of God, manifesting in the form of the birth of the child. The great writer and Nobel laureate, Rabindranath Tagore said that the birth of every child shows God's faith in mankind. Each child that is born can make a difference; can transform himself and his sphere of world. So look upon your child as a direct and clear manifestation of God's grace and understand that your child could become great. He has a vital role to play and you will be instrumental in enabling and empowering him or her to fulfill that role. He or she can become a great scientist, philosopher, artist, lawyer, politician or just a good human being and influence the lives of many.

जयतु ते शिशुर्जीवने सदा मधुरभावनो हर्षदायकः ।
जगति प्राप्नुयात्स्थानगौरवं पदमनुत्तमं मुक्तबन्धनः ॥२॥

jayatu te śiśur-jīvane sadā madhura-bhāvano harṣadāyakaḥ,
jagati prāpnuyāt-sthāna-gauravaṁ padam-anuttamaṁ muktabandhanaḥ (2)

2. May your child be ever successful in life, sweet natured and a giver of joy to all. May your child attain an honourable position in the world and find beatitude, free from all bondages.

Every parent wants their child to be happy, cheerful, sweet natured, well-behaved and brilliant and be a source of joy to all. Parents rejoice in the smallest achievements of their children and take great pride in their success. However we cannot guarantee that the child will be as they want him to be. But at least they should empower him and create the right ambience to enable it to happen.

It is sad to see young people the world over, falling prey to drugs and drink, indolence and indulgence, violence and crime. They waste their lives and destroy themselves – some also commit suicide. Such children only bring sorrow to all, especially their parents. Why do they go astray?

Herein we understand the importance of right upbringing (bāla-saṁvardhana). That is the duty and responsibility of the parents. It should not be considered a burden but a joyful duty which will need much patience but will bring immense joy and deep satisfaction. Our children are our future and we must invest enough time and right effort in their upbringing.

Some parents say that their life is very hectic and that they find no time for their children. Now that you have brought the child into this world, whose responsibility is his/her upbringing? Surely it cannot be totally dumped on the grandparents, maids, childcare centres, foster homes, schools or Bālavihārs. What love or commitment will a maid have in the upbringing of your child?

So how should you raise your children? A happy marriage will set the stage for the right upbringing of the child. The family is the foundation of the society and nation. A family in which there is mutual love and respect, sharing and caring, joy and laughter, learning and growing, will be the right ambience for the child's growth.

Also children have never been good at listening to their parents, but they never fail to imitate them. It is therefore important for you to 'mind your tongue' and 'watch your step' in front of your children. Be the role model for your child. Exemplify what you want them to be.

Many youngsters go astray because they have no inspiring/good role models or goals or find no meaningful purpose in life. They are quite often confused and misunderstand what constitutes a happy and successful life. You should guide your children in setting right, immediate and long-term goals which help him achieve the ultimate goal of life – freedom from all bondage.

The following verses describe eight aspects of parenting –

लालनं पालनं शिक्षा पोषणं कर्मकौशलम् ।
अर्पणं चैव संस्कारः पूर्णं जीवनदर्शनम् ॥१ ॥

lālanaṁ pālanaṁ śikṣā poṣaṇaṁ karmakauśalam,
arpaṇaṁ caiva saṁskāraḥ pūrṇaṁ jīvanadarśanam. (1)

1.Cuddling, protecting, educating, nourishing, inculcating efficiency, teaching dedication, imparting values and a holistic vision of life.

अङ्गान्येतानि सर्वाणि बालसंवर्धनस्य वै ।
पुष्यतां पितरौ बालान्मत्वा देवस्य पूजनम् ॥२ ॥

aṅgānyetāni sarvāṇi bālasaṁvardhanasya vai,
puṣyatāṁ pitarau bālān-matvā devasya pūjanam. (2)

2. All these constitute parenting. Parents should raise their children considering it as worship of God.

लालनं प्रेमवर्षा हि रक्षाभावस्तु पालनम् ।
शिक्षणं जीविकार्थं च पोषणं बलवर्धनम् ॥३ ॥

lālanaṁ premavarṣā hi rakṣābhāvastu pālanam,
śikṣaṇaṁ jīvikārthaṁ ca poṣaṇaṁ balavardhanam. (3)

3. Cuddling children is to shower love on them, protecting them is to give them a feeling of security,

educating them is to equip them with a means of earning their livelihood and nourishing them is to give them overall empowerment.

कौशलं सर्वकार्येषु नारायणसमर्पणम् ।
संस्कारः सद्गुणाधानं पूर्णमध्यात्मदर्शनम् ॥४ ॥

kauśalaṁ sarvakāryeṣu nārāyaṇa-samarpaṇam,
saṁskāraḥ sadguṇādhānaṁ pūrṇam-adhyātmadarśanam. (4)

4. Teaching them that – efficiency is all round dexterity, dedication is to offer oneself to God, saṁskāras are a strong value system, a holistic vision is a spiritual vision of life.

(1) Shower them with love: (lālanaṁ prema varṣā) – The literal meaning of lālanaṁ is to cuddle. Shower your child with love and affection. It is important that they feel loved and cared for. Express your love through your words and acts. Children that grow with parental love are secure and they in turn will love others. If they do not feel loved, they carry that insecurity all through their life.

(2) Develop a sense of security: (rakṣābhāvastu pālanam) – The child should feel protected by his parents. This will make him confident and fearless in facing life situations later on. This sense of security makes them open up to their parents and gives them the courage to confess even their follies to them. They then know that you will never leave them, come what may. A child was seen playing fearlessly when a ship was being violently rocked by the storm and there was panic everywhere. When asked why she was not scared, she said, 'Why should I be scared? My mother is here with me'.

Love and protection which creates a sense of security are especially important in the early stages of a child's life. It will create a close bond between you and then what you tell them will not fall on deaf ears.

(3) Educate for earning their livelihood: (śikṣaṇaṁ jīvikārthaṁ) – Provide your child with a holistic education which will make him/her a well integrated and well-rounded personality. Besides bringing literacy, education inculcates discipline, empowers him/her with knowledge and skill, develops their inherent talents and potential and enables them to earn their livelihood and become economically independent. 'Parents that do not educate their child are considered enemies because the child that is uneducated and uncultured never shines in the assembly of learned people and becomes a laughing stock'.[1]

(4) Nourish through empowerment: (poṣaṇaṁ balavardhanam) – Every child has an inherent talent and natural aptitude. The parents must help the child to discover this and cultivate it. They must nourish, encourage and empower the child so that he reaches his full potential. Besides physical nourishment, take tender care of his emotional, intellectual and spiritual growth.

Even if your child is challenged or with lesser potential, nourish him well. You will be surprised at the wonders possible with the right encouragement and empowerment. Little realising that the crowd was warning, a deaf child thought they were shouting words of encouragement and won a race! Many have not risen in life because there was no one to make them feel they could do it.

(5) Dexterity in action: (kauśalaṁ sarvakāryeṣu) – Teach your children to be efficient in all they do.

---

[1] *mātā śatru pitā vairi yena bāla na paṭhitā,*
na śobhate sabhā madhye haṁsa madhye bako yathā.

Encourage them to be neat in their work, prompt in their response, organised and knowledgeable. They need to also know all practical skills of life so that they can cope with various aspects of life. Your child may also have to learn how to cook, even if he has wonderful computer skills.

(6) Dedication of actions to an altar: (arpaṇaṁ nārāyaṇa-samarpaṇam) – An altar in life, alters your life. It is difficult to be continuously inspired, act with purpose and accept the results of actions gracefully and cheerfully without having an altar of dedication. The higher the altar of dedication, the greater is the transformation.

All great men were ordinary people till they found an altar of dedication. An ordinary barrister became the great Mahātmā Gandhi when he dedicated his life for the freedom of his country and the highest Truth. Śrī Gurudev Swami Chinmayananda would have remained only a good journalist but he joined the freedom struggle of India and later dedicated his life for the cultural and spiritual renaissance of the nation and transformed the lives of millions, the world over.

Inculcate this attitude of dedication in your children so that they use their God-given gifts in the service of the Lord, for a noble cause or in any noble field of action.

(7) Inculcating noble virtues: (saṁskāraḥ sadguṇādhānam) – Valuables are valuable, but values are invaluable. Value is what you respect, virtue is what you live. Inculcate good values and encourage your children to live them uncompromisingly till they become a habit and virtue. In life, if you do not stand for something, you fall for everything. Let your children know that the important things in life are not things. It is values like honesty, compassion, forgiveness and non-injury that sustain relationships, families, the society and the world. Lay a firm foundation of goodness in your child on which the superstructure of greatness can stand tall and unshaken by the temptations and trials of life.

(8) Holistic or spiritual view of life: (pūrṇamadhyātma-darśanam) – Teach your children to look upon life as a whole and live a holistic life. A lopsided, narrow or partial view of life will lead to sorrow.

A spiritual vision is holistic. You can view parenting also in the light of a spiritual vision. Khalil Gibran says, 'Children come through you, but do not belong to you!' They are God-given and you are given this special gift by God to take care and nurture them.

Make your child realise that he/she is potentially divine, a part of the Lord, a divine spark of Consciousness, God's special creation, born to fulfill his/her special role and attain perfection. A narrow vision is divisive, a broad vision is expansive and a divine vision is all-inclusive. Let your child grow up with a holistic and all-inclusive vision.

Parenting which includes the above will surely become deeply satisfying and joy giving.

Q & A on Marriage, Relationships and Parenting

Always go to the root of a problem. Symptomatic treatment only gives temporary relief but when the cause is removed the ailment is cured. You may seek advice for various challenges and situations that you face, but if you understand the very principle of spirituality and married life, then you will know what to do in all such challenges and situations.

However many a time people seek advice and wish to hear only what suits them and do not follow it if it is against their own preconceived ideas. Swami Jñānānanda, a monk from Kerala would ask, 'Will you follow my advice even if it is not what you want to hear or do?' So seek advice only from those you respect and trust and then follow it, no matter how difficult it is to do so.

Ques: How do you maintain a close relationship with your spouse, once you have children?

Ans: In fact the birth of the child itself is reason enough to bring you closer. Now you have a common locus of strong love, a binding factor called 'our child'. The love and respect for the 'mother of my child' or 'father of my child' is natural and can hold the couple together even in times of strained relationships. The spouse is instrumental in giving you your child who is God's gift to both to nurture and nourish together. Sharing your common responsibility should bring you closer.

Ques: When are my responsibilities as a parent complete and fulfilled towards my children?

Ans: The role of a parent is lifelong. However the nature of your responsibility changes in time. When your children are in school, you drive them but once they are eighteen they drive themselves and later in your old age, they may drive you around.

Your responsibility is to make them independent. You should not get psychologically dependent on they nor they on you, even though sometimes circumstances may make you physically or economically dependent.

Once they have become independent, then your role is only of an advisor, that too when they ask you.

Ques: When both parents are working and the children are put in day care, how does this impact the child's development?

Ans: Remember your child needs your presence and not your presents. He needs 'your care' not 'day care'. He needs to feel loved and secure – especially when he is young. The time you lose of his childhood cannot be made up later. You will never get to cuddle and watch him grow again. As a teenager he will not even allow you to touch him!

Ques: How can working parents achieve a balance of professional life with their parenting duties?

Ans: You have brought your child in this world, so you have to give him/her time also. This is more important in his/her infancy and early childhood. Money and career are important as is your child and family life. One spouse working or working part-time or working from home and so on are options available. So think of all available options, prioritise your goals and choose what is best for your child and his welfare.

Ques: How can we teach our children about dedication?

Ans: Teach them through your own example. That is the best. Also there are simple activities that they can be encouraged to do. For example, let them participate in sponsored walkathons or marathons, wherein the money they get is given to a noble cause. In Philippines in our Chinmaya Mission they have a children's club called SSS – Sacrifice, Save, Serve. The parent saves the money the child has earned by sacrificing his desire for an extra toy which is used to serve a poor child. All this will instill a spirit of dedication and service.

Ques: What do we do with a hyperactive child? How do we teach him dedication?

Ans: Don't ask him to meditate! His energy must be directed towards positive and productive activities. Otherwise he will become destructive. Since he already has a lot of energy and is active, all we need to do is motivate him to use it for a good cause he feels touched by. A child good at art painted hundreds of cards which he sold for the education of his poor friend. Touched by the scenes of destruction after the

Gujarat earthquake, Bilal, who was then only four and lived in Canada, sold oranges at street corners to make money for the victims of the earthquake. He has now gained international fame and jet sets around the world collecting funds for poor children the world over.

Ques: How do we ensure that children growing up in the West grow up with eastern (Indian) values and culture?

Ans: Practise them in your home. Respect your parents, be regular in your spiritual practice, be vegetarian and so on. Drop the idea that east is always better than the west and old is always better than the new. Everything stands on its own merit. Also teach them what is good in both cultures and what is common to all cultures and to follow universal values like honesty. Send them to the Chinmaya Mission Bālavihār classes. That is what we teach in these weekly classes for children.

Ques: What can we do for the child when he/she is in the womb?

Ans: The child starts learning from the womb. Your thoughts, words and actions affect him/her even in the womb. Live a disciplined and spiritual life. The mother should be kept cheerful and happy, that is the father's job! Strong negative emotions, unhealthy diet and entertainment will affect the child adversely.

Ques: How do we find time for spirituality in our busy householder's life?

Ans: This question arises because we consider spirituality as a particular action. Spirituality is not doing something different or special. It is in doing everything in a special way with a special attitude. For that you do not need separate time.

You need time for doing yoga or for singing, but you do not need special time for being honest, good, friendly or helpful. You can be these whilst doing everything. So never say that I have no time for spirituality.

As long as you make a division between spiritual life and householder's life, there will be a conflict. The spiritual attitude must pervade your householder life – professional, personal or social. Serve the world as worship of God. Make your work, your worship. As already mentioned, parenting can also be considered as an opportunity given by God to nurture and nourish His special gift to us.

Also devote some time each day for spiritual practices. You may not have much time, but 15 minutes to half an hour each day can be devoted to meditation, prayer, worship or study of the scriptures. This will tune and fine-tune your mind and empower you with the right attitude and the positive energy to work the whole day. 75% time of a householder goes in taking care of family and work. When he/she retires they can devote 75% of their time to spiritual practices and a sannyāsin or monk can devote his whole life for meditation and seeking God-realisation. Spiritual practices purify your mind and prepare it for higher achievements.

Ques: How can I please other people like my husband? Sometimes I feel I am not doing the right thing, but I do it because I want to please someone or because of external pressure. What should I do?

Ans: This reminds me of a joke. A lady asked her friend, "Is it difficult to please your husband?" She replied, "I don't know, I have never tried!"

First of all, remember that it is difficult to please another person. A lady who was told that the way to a man's heart is through his stomach, spent most of her time cooking. This irritated her husband to the limit and he complained, 'She does nothing except cook all day!'

Secondly, try to do what pleases the other person, not what you think should please them. Get to know the person's likes and dislikes and do not rub them the wrong way. A wife uninterested in football is not likely to be pleased by the gift of tickets to a 'Premier League Football' match, however costly they may be.

Thirdly, instead of doing what will please yourself or the other person, do what is right and do what is good to do. In trying to gratify oneself or another, we might land up doing what is immoral, illegal or unjust. Doing what is right may not please the other person, but it is best for all in the long run. A child may be pleased by bunking school or underaged driving but it would be best not to allow him his wrong ways.

Sometimes inner compulsions or outer pressure may force us to do wrong. If you give in to these pressures you will have to bear the consequences. At least become aware, minimize the compromises, do not make them into a habit and stick to your decisions as far as possible.

Ques: I believe in God, pray for a long time everyday and read the Guru-caritra. But I do not do any chanting or worship. Is that alright?

Ans: Any soap can be used to wash the body. Similarly any spiritual practice that helps us to purify and tune up the mind is fine. Do not do the spiritual practices mechanically. What is important is to feel the presence of God all the time.

A teacher gave his two disciples a fruit each and asked them to eat it in a place where none would see them. One returned soon, but another came hours later with the fruit in hand saying, 'Every place I went, there was someone – plant, animal or human life. There where no one else was present, I realised that I am watching myself and there is also God!'

Also our belief should be strong. If we truly believe in God there should be no worry in our life. If we know that God is omniscient, omnipotent and all-compassionate, will He not take care of us? Feel His presence and have faith. Lengthy or superficially done rituals, without these, will not be very effective.

Ques: I am in search of a Guru who can guide me to attain Self-realisation. How do I search or will it happen on its own?

Ans: A Guru is required if you have true desire for knowledge. How intense is your desire? If your desire is intense, you will see that you keep on getting right guidance and opportunities to learn. Make use of all such opportunities to know the Truth. You focus your mind on increasing the demand, the supply shall happen.

Ques: You have said that our mutual love should grow each day. How do we do that?

Ans: Do not let the romance die after marriage. Find new ways to please each other. Discover new aspects of your spouse and form a deeper emotional, intellectual and spiritual relationship. Focus your attention on the positive aspects of the other person and do not let little negative irritants erode your love. Instead of thinking he presses the toothpaste from the middle or she keeps snoring so loudly, think he is always there when I need him or she takes such good care of the children.

When you both focus on giving, then the love grows. When you focus on getting, love erodes. Love the person in spite of his/her weakness, then even their eccentricities will increase your love. A wife knowing that the husband would forget her birthday brought herself a costly present and told him lovingly, 'Now all you need to do is pay the bill!'

Ques: In marriage, what is more important – love, respect or trust?

Ans: Trust is the most important. Love and respect flourish when there is strong faith and falter when doubt and suspicion creep in.

Ques: If true freedom is to be able to give up all, how can we carry on with our family responsibilities?

Ans: True freedom is to be detached from within, not just give up outside things and walk out of responsibilities and duties. Of course if the need arises, we should also be able to give up and walk away!

Ques: We are both Hindus but belong to different religious sects (sampradāyas). What should a couple do, especially how should they bring up their children in these circumstances?

Ans: It is interesting that when the boy and girl fall in love, these differences don't seem to matter. After marriage these differences become suddenly very important. Life is all about adjusting, especially married life. Both must learn to live and let live, understand and respect each other's beliefs. Discover the common essence of 'Dharma' and give freedom to the other to follow their ways of practice. Children too will pick up the essence of both practices when the common principles are emphasised.

Sometimes however the one with a weaker belief yields to the one with a stronger belief. A wife was seen wearing a T-shirt which read, 'One Way'. The husband's T-shirt read, 'Your Way'. Someone observed that a family lived very peacefully. When questioned how they did so, he said, "She decides all home affairs – how to raise the children, where to go on vacation, what school the children will go to, to whom they will pray and so on. I deal with international affairs – Wimbledon finals, the Palestinian problem, global warming and so on. We have no common grounds of conflict!"

Ques: How do we balance our duties to serve the society with our duties to raise our children?

Ans: It is not necessary that all your work and talent be used only in making money. Once you understand that you will have more time for your children and the society, spend quality time with your children at home, involve them also wherever possible in service to society and use your time, money and talent in contributing to making the world a better place. A lady I know sells her paintings and contributes the amount to the Chinmaya Mission.

Ques: What is our responsibility towards our parents in India as we stay far away from them?

Ans: If you cannot go back to take care of them, call them here. If that is not agreeable to them, arrange others – siblings or relations – to care for them. Otherwise at least take care of their comforts and economic needs and visit them as often as possible.

Many parents prefer not to uproot themselves from India in old age. Many wish to lead a peaceful retired life in their native place and pursue their spiritual goals. It is the duty of the children to love, respect, help and care for them whether from far or near and not burden them with the task of raising their own grand children.

Ques: After a conflict or making a mistake it is often hard to be gracious or ask for forgiveness. How can we become more gracious and learn to apologise?

Ans: It is our ego that does not allow us to be gracious or apologise for our mistakes. I have kept this management principle in mind whilst dealing with Mission matters and also relationships and it has helped me. It is called the KISS principle – keep it simple and straight.

- Life is complicated enough, without you adding your ego to it. Remember you are not omniscient. If you don't know, admit it.
- If you need help, ask for it.
- If you commit a mistake, apologise. Do not hesitate or delay.

When I was a student in the āśrama, each of us was asked to speak on a topic. Since we were so close, we all knew each other's faults. One student indirectly spoke about my faults in his talk. Everyone knew whom he was referring to. I got angry and decided to expose his faults when my turn came. Then I realised that what he said had some truth in it and so I went and touched his feet and thanked him for pointing out my faults. He was surprised and became apologetic and we became best of friends. To react and behave in an ungracious way is not spiritual. Whenever I have said something in reaction, I call the other person and apologise and our relations are maintained and many times strengthened. Be genuine in your apology.

Also be forgiving of other's faults and forgive them when they apologise. A husband apologised for his mistake. The wife kept reminding him about it saying, 'I have forgiven you but not forgotten and I do not want you to forget that I have forgiven'.

Ques: How can one be compassionate towards oneself?

Ans: Be like Lord Śiva who has three eyes - the two eyes of justice and compassion and the third eye of discrimination or knowledge. Do not be too harsh, judgmental or condemning towards your own faults. Do not look down on yourself or curse yourself. At the same time, do not be too indulgent and soft about your faults. Do not keep justifying or finding excuses. We must use discrimination and wisdom to understand when to be firm and when and how much to be compassionate towards oneself. This will come by increasing one's spiritual strength by regular study of scriptures, prayer and meditation. The prayer of serenity is most beautiful – 'God give me the courage to change what I can, serenity to accept what I cannot and the wisdom to understand the difference'. Be wise and compassionate.

Ques: What is your advice to a young couple that wants to lead a life of celibacy and devote their life to spiritual practices? There is pressure from the parents to have children and they say that spirituality is for old age. Will we be doing something wrong?

Ans: If you are both very firm and convinced, do not yield to any pressure. If you are very sure that you wish to lead a spiritual life, do so completely.

For those who are not very firm or sure, it is best to lead a normal householder's life and have children. They should then look upon their children as a gift of God and lead a spiritual life. Spirituality is not just for old age or for sannyāsins or monks. You can pursue a spiritual life remaining in the midst of worldly activity. With a spiritual vision, carry on your family life.

Ques: Why is there so much possessiveness in a husband wife relationship?

Ans: This is true. You are more willing to share your other possessions but never your spouse. You do not like it when anyone especially any man or woman is possessive of your spouse. When each is confident of the other's total love and commitment towards the other, the possessiveness does not become obsessive or problematic and the relationship is healthy. The basis of relationship should be spiritual and not just physical, emotional or material.

Ques: We are told that we should realise the Truth. What is the Truth and how can we realise It?

Ans: God/Truth is your own true nature, your inner Self. Your entire life should be geared towards this realisation. Prepare your mind through selfless and unconditional performance of your duties, dedicating all your actions towards a noble goal, regular worship, prayer, study and meditation. This will lead you to deeper reflection and enquiry into the nature of the Truth and finally the realisation of your infinite Self.

Ques: I worry about the eventual mortality of my old parents even though I know it is inevitable. How can I overcome my worry?

Ans: Remember, we too are mortal and may pass away any day, not just our parents. Do your best to make your parents happy and comfortable now. Spend your time in serving and caring for them. When you do your best for them now, you can leave the rest (worry) in God's care.

Ques: How can we make our children spiritual minded and when should we start?

Ans: First of all, you become spiritual minded. Children will imbibe your values and follow your actions. A lady took her young son to a saint complaining that he ate too many sweets and that it was harmful to him. The saint asked them to return after a month. After a month, when they met him, he said, “Dear child, do not eat so many sweets, it will harm you”. The boy instantly promised that he would stop eating sweets. The mother asked the saint, why the same advice was not given a month back. The saint said, “I too was eating too many sweets a month back and so had no moral right to advice the child”. He had given up eating sweets and then he told the child to do so. Then alone his words had the power to change the child.

You become spiritual and the children shall learn from your attitude and behavior.

May God’s grace and Pūjya Gurudev’s blessings be on all.

Om Tat Sat

Other books by Swami Tejomayananda